HOPKINS

—

THE MYSTIC POETS

HOPKINS

—

THE MYSTIC POETS

Preface by Rev. Thomas Ryan, CSP,
author of *Prayer of Heart and Body*

Walking Together, Finding the Way
SKYLIGHT PATHS Publishing

Hopkins:
The Mystic Poets

© 2004 by SkyLight Paths Publishing

For information regarding permission to reprint material from this book, please write or fax your request to SkyLight Paths Publishing, Permissions Department, at the address / fax number listed below, or e-mail your request to permissions@skylightpaths.com.

Library of Congress Cataloging-in-Publication Data

Hopkins, Gerard Manley, 1844–1889.
Hopkins : the mystic poets / preface by Thomas Ryan.
p. cm. — (The mystic poets series)
Includes bibliographical references and indexes.
ISBN 1-59473-010-5 (hc)
ISBN 978-1-68336-115-2 (pbk)
1. Mysticism—Poetry. I. Title. II. Series.
PR4803.H44A6 2004
821'.8—dc22

2004003565

SkyLight Paths Publishing is creating a place where people of different spiritual traditions come together for challenge and inspiration, a place where we can help each other understand the mystery that lies at the heart of our existence.

SkyLight Paths sees both believers and seekers as a community that increasingly transcends traditional boundaries of religion and denomination—people wanting to learn from each other, *walking together, finding the way.*

SkyLight Paths, "Walking Together, Finding the Way" and colophon are trademarks of LongHill Partners, Inc., registered in the U.S. Patent and Trademark Office.

Walking Together, Finding the Way
Published by SkyLight Paths Publishing
An imprint of Turner Publishing Company
4507 Charlotte Avenue, Suite 100
Nashville, TN 37209
Tel: (615) 255-2665
www.skylightpaths.com

Contents

Preface

Rev. Thomas Ryan, CSP

Gerard Manley Hopkins (1844–1889) was born into an English Anglican family, became a Roman Catholic, and entered the Jesuits. Each of these three formative elements contributed in its own way to the development of his human capacity for mysticism.

Hopkins the English Anglican

Just as being born an Anglican in Africa or India would shape one's soul in a particular way, so does being born as an Anglican in England. Gerard's parents were devoted to the Church and reverenced the scriptures. From them he inherited a proud tradition of education in literature and the arts. His father, head of a firm of actuaries, had himself published verse, and his mother was known for her artistic temperament and talent. Gerard, the eldest of nine children, grew up learning to draw and paint, write and play music. His imagination received early and rich development; already in grammar school he was the proud recipient of a poetry prize.

These skills, early learned, would serve him well in

years to come. In his later journals, meticulous illustrations of flowers, trees, and waves adorn the pages, revealing an artist's eye. His musical intuitions would eventually shape his verse with an effective use of echo, alliteration, and repetition in what he himself described as a "sprung rhythm" that lent intensity, vibrancy, and flexibility to the lines of his poems.

The human imagination has the power to capture realities that can be expressed in no other way than imaginatively, and one certainly sees in Hopkins's poetry a fertile and active imagination. The Swiss psychologist Carl Jung opined that symbolic language is the first language of the psyche. So rich is Hopkins's use of that symbolic language that to this day critical opinion is still divided as to the precise meaning of his poem "The Windhover." Is it a mere nature poem, celebrating the beauty and mastery of a bird, or is it an ecstatic rejoicing in the beauty of Christ, known first in the bird and then in the Christian knight's heart?

As William Countryman has recently shown in his book *The Poetic Imagination: An Anglican Spiritual Tradition,* there is a long and rich tradition in English literature of using the lyric as a vehicle for spiritual discourse. Lyric serves many purposes, but one of its most ancient and enduring functions is to celebrate love. Spirituality and love have much in common: they are both interior, consensual, and relational.

Many people of religion think of their tradition's

holy writ when they hear the word "revelation," but there is another locus of God's revelation in Celtic spirituality, and that is the created world. The Bible is the "small book"; the world of nature is the "big book." Both reveal the Creator. The order of creation actually fulfills a role in salvation by turning the soul toward liberating intimacy with God.

The transparency of nature to God became something of an article of faith in the English-speaking world after the romantic poets like Wordsworth and Coleridge. Nature, they felt, is as good a language for spirituality as sacred scripture. This is precisely the contribution that artistic pursuits make to our human growth and development as inspired flesh: poetry and art and music seize upon the human experience in ways that reveal new possibilities of intimacy with the Divine. In the way they reach out and grab us by the heart at unexpected times, they reaffirm that the Holy will meet us when it chooses, in "pied beauty": "Glory be to God" for "rose-moles all in stipple upon trout that swim."

The Anglican spiritual and literary tradition of nature as revelation left its clear imprint upon Hopkins, as evidenced by these lines from "Inversnaid":

> What would the world be, once bereft
> Of wet and of wildness? Let them be left,
> O let them be left, wildness and wet;
> Long live the weeds and the wilderness yet.

Hopkins the Roman Catholic

After three years of study at Balliol College, Oxford, where he had won a grant and continued writing poetry while studying classics, at age twenty-two Hopkins was received into the Catholic Church by John Henry Newman, a leading light in the Oxford Movement, which renewed interest in the relationship between Anglicanism and Roman Catholicism.

The mystical tradition of the Latin Western Church opened to him a treasure trove of offerings. As a classics student he would have learned that the very word "mystery" in the New Testament comes from the Greek *mysterion* and refers to the hidden presence of God and Christ in the scriptures, in the sacraments, and in the events of daily life. The import of its derivatives like "mysticism," "mystical," and "mystic," with their focus on the human potential for immediate experience of the Divine, would have resonated with a young man who had already demonstrated the careful observation of a painter's eye in verse written with sensuous intensity.

In the Catholic tradition of Christian faith, mysticism is essentially a deeply human life. It is not reserved for an elite. The human person is mystical by nature, that is, experientially referred to a holy, loving Mystery. For Karl Rahner, one of the most noted Roman Catholic theologians of the twentieth century, there is at the heart of every human's existence what he called the "transcendental existential": in our very existence we are turned toward the

Transcendent. We are "open outwards" toward the Divine, hard-wired for communion with God.

This inbuilt capacity for transcendence, for mysticism, can be expressed in silent hope in the face of death; in radical fidelity to the depths of one's conscience even when one appears like a fool before others; in forgiveness without the expectation of being rewarded; in faithful service and loving sacrifice; and in unreserved love for another. All these make up the wider mysticism in daily living. A loving, transforming Mystery created all things, communicated to all things, and embraces all things. There can be, therefore, a mysticism of everyday things like working, eating, talking, and, as Hopkins describes in "The Alchemist in the City," simply walking and looking:

> I walk my breezy belvedere
> To watch the low or levant sun,
> I see the city pigeons veer,
> I mark the tower swallows run

The importance Catholicism gives to the sacramental principle is one of its most distinctive features. The sacramental principle springs from Christian faith in the incarnation of the Word of God in Jesus. In him the invisible and transcendent took on visible and tangible form. Ever since, matter has been permeated with divinizing energies. A sacrament, or sign of an encounter with the Divine, always involves something concrete and visible, like water, wine, bread, oil.

The traditional Catholic emphasis on sacraments

underlines the conviction that God comes to us not in a purely spiritual and invisible way but rather through visible, concrete, tangible, earthy things and in the context of community. Sacraments presuppose and give expression to a certain understanding of human life. They presume that we are not burdened with bodies from which our souls will one day gleefully find release, but that we are by God's design embodied spirits and that this materiality, this very sensuous and enspirited flesh, is the place God chose to call "home." We do not just *have* a body; we *are* our bodies.

Analogously, all matter has a sacramental character. In becoming incarnate in Jesus of Nazareth, the Word in some way drew close not only to all humans, but to all creation, giving everything a deeper dignity and a more intimate relationship with God. Everything reflects something of the beauty and life-affirming energy of God. By both nature and grace we are sacraments for one another, visible signs and tangible expressions of the mystery that grounds and permeates all of life. Hopkins therefore found a ready complement between the Anglican spiritual tradition of nature-as-revelation and the Roman Catholic sacramental sense of the majesty and mystery of creation.

Hopkins the Jesuit

When Hopkins died of typhoid fever at forty-five, among his unfinished works was a commentary on the

Spiritual Exercises of St. Ignatius of Loyola, founder of the Jesuit order. Here, too, Hopkins found fuel for his fire, for Ignatian spirituality and mysticism also finds God in all things in order to love and serve God in all things. It is a mysticism of joy in the world, which serves God in and through this world. It is an Easter spirituality that loves the earth because the Trinitarian God creates, redeems, and loves it. It is a spirituality that would assert "the world is charged with the grandeur of God."

The directives in the *Spiritual Exercises* are meant to ensure that the reader fully uses the senses, emotions, passions, fantasy, memory, reason, intellect, heart, and will in order to interiorize the material of the exercise. In praying with a biblical passage that presents Christ preaching from the bow of a boat to a crowd on the shore, for example, the person is instructed to make a mental image of the place and to see, hear, taste, smell, and touch in imagination what is occurring. One is encouraged to give vent to spontaneous feelings and desires and to ask for tears, sorrow, affectionate love, joy, gladness, peace, and tranquility. Ignatius's mystical union with the Trinity did not incline him away from the senses and the world, but toward it. The *Spiritual Exercises* offer one of the clearest and most influential expositions of the affirmative path in Christian spirituality.

Other currents of spirituality were certainly present in Hopkins's day, as well, that were less affirmative of God's grandeur in creation and more suspicious of human sentiment and embodiment. It was perhaps his contact with these that led him to burn his poetry upon entering the Jesuits in a zealous misperception that artistic activity would not be consistent with a religious vocation. Eventually he shed this mistaken piety, and his poetic soul responded with resilience to the glories of the mysteries of faith he was studying in theology. It was his own Jesuit superior who encouraged him to write a poem about a shipwreck that had moved him profoundly— "The Wreck of the Deutschland"—involving the drowning of five German Franciscan nuns in the incoming tide at the mouth of the Thames. In the poem he concentrates on one tall nun who calls over the storm throughout the night, "Christ, Christ, come quickly."

Because Christianity believes in an all-transcendent God who becomes incarnate, mystical experience is both negative and positive, personal and impersonal, characterized by divine darkness and an experience of the other as Friend or Lover. It travels, one might say, by both a night train and a day train. The day train sees and affirms God in all creation. The night train's passage is in darkness and unknowing, requiring one to journey in blind faith that "something is out there even though I can't see it or name it." Both trains deliver one to the station, and both require investment in a ticket of loving service.

Hopkins's poems indicate that during his years of study and pastoral work in England, he traveled largely on the day train. W. H. Gardner, the editor of an earlier collection of Hopkins's poetry, characterizes the verse written during his years of theological studies (1875–1877) as "poems of nature and God," and those penned during seven subsequent years of pastoral work as a missioner and parish priest in various Jesuit churches in London, Oxford, Liverpool, and Glasgow (1877–1883) as "poems of God and man." Hopkins's favorite devotion—to the heart of Christ—reveals his love affair with the Christ who "plays in ten thousand places/Lovely in limbs, and lovely in eyes not his."

But when he was appointed as professor of Greek literature at University College, Dublin, in 1884, Hopkins's ride on the night train commenced. He was not happy in Ireland, apparently overworked and in poor health. Gardner describes his writing during this period as "poems of desolation and recovery," as in these lines from the poem called "Carrion Comfort":

> The hero whose heaven-handling flung me, fóot
> tród
> Me? or me that fought him? O which one? is it
> each one?
>   That night, that year
> Of now done darkness I wretch lay wrestling with
> (my God!)
>   my God.

In summary, I would say that insofar as mysticism is *Christian,* there must be incarnational, affirmative, day train elements. And insofar as it is mysticism, there must be negative, night train elements that strip one of the supports previously relied upon and bring one in one's naked being into the presence of the ever-greater God. For Hopkins, this seemed to take the form of spiritual aridity and artistic frustration. In the final year of his short life, he wrote in "Thou art indeed just, Lord,"

> birds build—but not I build; no, but strain,
> Time's eunuch, and not breed one work that wakes.
> Mine, O thou lord of life, send my roots rain.

During his own lifetime, his poems were read only in manuscript by his friends and a few fellow poets. The first collected edition did not see the light of day until 1918, twenty-nine years after his death. It was only with the second edition in 1930 that Hopkins's work was recognized as among the most original, powerful, and influential literary accomplishments of his century.

It is both our privilege and our pleasure to read his poems today.

Rev. Thomas Ryan, CSP

Who Is Gerard Manley Hopkins?

Gerard Manley Hopkins lived a relatively short but passionate life. He was a lover of the natural world, seeing the Divine throughout all aspects of creation. He also had a relationship with Jesus Christ that seems at times to be so intimate as to remind us only of those women mystics from the late Middle Ages who emphasized their spiritual union with Christ. His verse displays remarkable abilities to not only see the world in original ways, but to *express* that mysticism in fresh language and startling metaphor, as well.

Readers today can use Hopkins's particular grounding in Christianity as a "window" through which we might "see" the Divine Presence in the world around us. The poet's relationship with the mystical Jesus is his own way of spiritual connection with the physical world around him. Your way may be different, but Hopkins's images and vitality can still kindle your path. Hopkins's sermons, his journals and letters, and his remarkably impassioned poetry all attest to his vision of God as present in the universe, and we should not read him exclusively as a literary figure. His verse is lovely (at times), but that is almost beside the point. These ideas and expressions are ways of seeing the Divine anew, for people of all faiths and backgrounds.

Hopkins was a convert to Roman Catholicism, having grown up in a traditional, middle-class Anglican home outside of London. While a student at Oxford, at age twenty-two, he joined the Roman Catholic Church—which was a very unpopular move to make at that time in England—and within two years entered the Order of the Society of Jesus (the Jesuits), beginning nine years of study and preparation before priestly ordination.

He is unique in the history of English-language religious poetry, as his verses do not read like those of one trying to impress anyone in the Church. They communicate a searching soul, and a spirit at times quiet in the world, at other times stirred up. One early critic characterized Hopkins's poetic style this way, comparing him with the great British devotional poet and parish priest George Herbert: "Pope said of Herbert that he wrote 'like a gentleman, for his own amusement.' Hopkins wrote like a devotee offering a sacrifice."[1]

Hopkins's poems were not published until nearly thirty years following his death in 1889. Another poet, one of the most renowned of his time, Robert Bridges, gathered them together for the first time and added his own critical notes about their contents. The *Times Literary Supplement*—the venerable literary review in London—published a review of the edited poems a few months after the publication. The reviewer explained how one should read a Hopkins poem:

> In 1876 he wrote a poem, "The Wreck of the Deutschland," [see p. 71] which is still more novel than the most novel poems of today. Mr. Bridges

calls it a great dragon folded in the gate to forbid all entrance; and, indeed, it is difficult. For Hopkins poetry meant difficulty; he wrote it to say more than could be said otherwise; it was for him a packing of words with sense, both emotional and intellectual. The defect of the newest English poetry is that it says too little. Our young poets seem determined to make their art too easy, at least for themselves, to reduce it to expletives. But Hopkins went further than any other poet known to us from common speech. In all his more difficult poems there are several ordinary poems assumed, both their ideas and their metre; and on these assumptions, which the reader is expected to make, he builds his own poem. It is like that modern music which assumes the conventions of older music and departs from them, still using them as the basis of departure. But Hopkins' verse is more difficult even than that music because it assumes that the reader grasps the sense of what is unsaid. He begins where most poets leave off, not out of affectation, but because he wishes to go further.

A Short Introduction to Hopkins's Mysticism

Always the world was fresh to him, as it is fresh to children and to the very mature.... Few men have loved nature more rapturously than he; fewer still with such a youthful and perennial curiosity. There is a tender excitement in his attitude toward natural beauty (whether treated incidentally or as a parable) that is very contagious.... Nature, indeed, was his one secular inspiration.

—KATHERINE BREGY, WRITING FOR THE
AMERICAN MAGAZINE *CATHOLIC WORLD* (1909)

Gerard Manley Hopkins is the poet of Anglicans and Roman Catholics, of spiritual seekers who have been disenfranchised by Christianity, of nature-lovers, and many others. His play with words—love of the ways that words sound—sets him apart from other poets who focus primarily on spirituality. Hopkins doesn't preach; we watch him as he wrestles and yearns.

Hopkins was clearly a Christian, and much of his imagery expresses a relationship to God in Christ in new ways. But again, unlike the works of many religious poets, Hopkins's poems are rarely easy.

Sometimes even the grammar is implied; its skeleton is not there—you have to imagine it there. The words succeed each other without it, each one

15

bringing a new inrush of sense into the sentence, which hardly exists; and each inrush would in ordinary prose, or even verse, need a whole sentence to itself. Here is an example, not the most extreme, from "The Wreck of the Deutschland." The subject is Christ:

> I admire thee, master of the tides,
> Of the Yore-flood, of the year's fall;
> The recurb and the recovery of the gulf's sides,
> The girth of it and the wharf of it and the wall;
> Stanching, quenching ocean of a motionable mind;
> Ground of being, and granite of it; past all
> Grasp God, throned behind
> Death with a sovereignty that heeds but hides, bodes but abides;[2]

The same reviewer who wrote those words in the *Catholic World,* above, enthusiastic at the first appearance of Hopkins's poems thirty years after the poet's death, explained to readers:

The whole book thrills with spirit, a spirit that does not disdain sense but heightens it. The poems are crowded with objects sharply cut, and with sounds no less sharp and clashing; you fight your way through the verses, yet they draw you on. There is beauty everywhere without luxury, the beauty that seems to come of painful intense watching, the utter, disinterested delight of one who sees another world, not through, but in this one. It is as if he heard everywhere a music too difficult, because too beautiful, for our ears and noted down what he could catch of it; authentic fragments that we trust even when they bewilder us.[3]

This is what awaits the reader of Hopkins's poetry: "beauty that seems to come of painful intense watching" brought to us by "one who sees another world, not through, but in this one."

Hopkins is a poet of the spirit, but he is also one of our greatest innovators when it comes to seeing the natural world. For example, in his unique vision,

Snow is "wiry and white-fiery" and "whirlwind-swivelled."
Clouds become "silk-sacks."
Stars are "circle-citadels."
Violent seas are "rash smart sloggering brine."

Sometimes the words themselves do not make sense, but the combination of words, and the sound of them, does.

Dawn is imaged in "the bent world's brink."
The riverbank, "wind-wandering weed-winding."

The images can tire a reader out, but they are also thrilling new ways of seeing things.

Hopkins's mysticism also combines these two themes: love for the natural world and passion for Christ.

Hopkins refers to Jesus using images of creation: "womb-of-all, home-of-all"; he refers to Christ as Savior as "our passion-plungèd giant risen." Many books have been written about this Jesuit's unusual love and attachment for Jesus Christ, as seen in the images of his poems. Most directly he united his love for the natural world—and his vision of it—with his greater beloved, Christ. Like William Blake before him, Hopkins had mystical visions of God in the natural world.

When reading the poems, we may sometimes wonder if the world Hopkins inhabited was the same one as our own. How do mystics see the natural world and the Divine as so completely intertwined? How can we live in the earthly world yet be ever conscious of the presence of God? An insight into the answer is offered in a journal entry that Hopkins wrote in September 1870. After a lyrical description of his first sight of the northern lights, he continued: "This busy working of nature wholly independent of the earth and seeming to go on in a strain of time not reckoned by our reckoning of days and years but simpler and as if correcting the preoccupation of the world by being preoccupied with and appealing to and dated to the day of judgment was like a new witness to God and filled me with delightful fear." For Hopkins and mystics like him, from Hafiz to Blake to Sri Ramakrishna, all creation led to the Divine.

Another early reviewer of the first edition of Hopkins's published poems explained it this way:

This solemn rapture and awe is one characteristic note of his mysticism. The other, not unconnected with it, is the avoidance of human imagery, the tendency to escape from the personal to the spatial. A natural Platonist, it is plain that he discovers God most easily through the beauty and life of the physical universe: Christ behind "the piece-bright paling" of the stars, the Holy Ghost brooding on "the bent world's brink" at dawn, even Mary in the "world-mothering air." This mood, this vision, appears again and again: because of it, for him, "There lives the dearest freshness deep down things."[4]

Perhaps Hopkins's most famous lines are these that demonstrate his personal vision for God in the world:

> The world is charged with the grandeur of God.
>   It will flame out, like shining from shook foil.

Theologians would explain this as a sacramental view of God in the world. Beyond the traditional seven sacraments of the Catholic Church, Hopkins added a mystical perspective on the incarnation of God in Christ. Just as Jesus Christ took on a human body and was fully God and fully human at the same time, Hopkins believed that the incarnation of God reiterates what occurred in the original creation: God became present in the world around us. Matter and spirit are all mixed up together. Hopkins offers new language with which we might see the world in this sacramental way.

Excerpts from His Sermons

The Physical Beauty of Jesus Christ

(From "Christ Our Hero," preached Sunday evening, November 23, 1879. Text: Luke 2:33)

There met in Jesus Christ all things that can make man lovely and loveable. In his body he was most beautiful. This is known first by the tradition in the Church that it was so and by holy writers agreeing to suit those words to him. "Thou art beautiful in mould above the sons of men": we have even accounts of him written in early times. They tell us that he was moderately tall, well built and slender in frame, his features straight and beautiful, his hair inclining to auburn, parted in the midst, curling and clustering about the ears and neck as the leaves of a filbert, so they speak, upon the nut. He wore also a forked beard and this as well as the locks upon his head were never touched by razor or shears; neither, his health being perfect, could a hair ever fall to the ground. The account I have been quoting (it is from memory, for I cannot now lay my hand upon it) we do not indeed for certain know to be correct, but it has been current in the Church and many generations have drawn our Lord accordingly either in their own minds or in his images.

Another proof of his beauty may be drawn from the words *proficiebat sapientia et aetate et gratia apud Deum et homines* (Luc. ii 52). "He went forward in wisdom and bodily frame and favour with God and men"; that is, he pleased both God and men daily more and more by his growth of mind and body. But he could not have pleased by growth of body unless the body was strong, healthy, and beautiful that grew. But the best proof of all is this, that his body was the special work of the Holy Ghost. He was not born in nature's course, no man was his father; had he been born as others are he must have inherited some defect of figure or of constitution, from which no man born as fallen men are born is wholly free unless God interfere to keep him so. But his body was framed directly from heaven by the power of the Holy Ghost, of whom it would be unworthy to leave any the least botch or failing in his work. So the first Adam was moulded by God himself and Eve built up by God too out of Adam's rib and they could not but be pieces, both, of faultless workmanship: the same then and much more must Christ have been.

His constitution too was tempered perfectly, he had neither disease nor the seeds of any: weariness he felt when he was wearied, hunger when he fasted, thirst when he had long gone without drink, but to the touch of sickness he was a stranger. I leave it to you, brethren, then to picture him, in whom the fullness of the godhead dwelt bodily, in his bearing how majestic, how strong and yet how lovely and lissome in his limbs, in his look how earnest, grave but kind. In his Passion all this strength was spent, this lissomness crippled, this beauty wrecked, this majesty beaten down. But now it is more than all restored, and for myself I make no secret I look forward with eager desire to seeing the matchless beauty of Christ's body in the heavenly light.

The Mind and Character of Jesus

(From "Christ Our Hero," preached Sunday evening, November 23, 1879. Text: Luke 2:33)

[Jesus] was the greatest genius that ever lived. You know what genius is, brethren—beauty and perfection in the mind. For perfection in the bodily frame distinguishes a man among other men his fellows: so may the mind be distinguished for its beauty above other minds and that is genius. Then when this genius is duly taught and trained, that is wisdom; for without training genius is imperfect and again wisdom is imperfect without genius. But Christ, we read, advanced in wisdom and in favour with God and men: now this wisdom, in which he excelled all men, had to be founded on an unrivalled genius. Christ then was the greatest genius that ever lived.

You must not say, Christ needed no such thing as genius; his wisdom came from heaven, for he was God. To say so is to speak like the heretic Apollinaris, who said that Christ had indeed a human body but no soul, he needed no mind and soul, for his godhead, the Word of God, that stood for mind and soul in him. No, but Christ was perfect man and must have mind as well as body and that mind was, no question, of the rarest excellence and beauty; it was genius. As Christ lived and breathed and moved in a true and not a phantom human body and in that labored, suffered, was crucified, died, and was buried; as he merited by acts of his human will; so he reasoned and planned and invented by acts of his own human genius, genius made perfect by wisdom of its own, not the divine wisdom only.

A witness to his genius we have in those men who being sent to arrest him came back empty-handed, spellbound by his eloquence, saying "Never man spoke like this man."

A better proof we have in his own words, his Sermon on the Mount, his parables, and all his sayings recorded in the Gospel. My brethren, we are so accustomed to them that they do not strike us as they do a stranger that hears them first, else we too should say, "Never man etc." No stories or parables are like Christ's, so bright, so pithy, so touching; no proverbs or sayings are such jewellery: they stand off from other men's thoughts like stars, like lilies in the sun; nowhere in literature is there anything to match the Sermon on the Mount: if there is let men bring it forward.

Time does not allow me to call your minds to proofs or instances. Besides Christ's sayings in the Gospels a dozen or so more have been kept by tradition and are to be found in the works of the Fathers and early writers and one even in the Scripture itself: "It is more blessed etc." When these sayings are gathered together, though one cannot feel sure of every one, yet reading all in one view they make me say, "These must be Christ's, never man etc." One is: Never rejoice but when you look upon your brother in love. Another is: My mystery is for me and for the children of my house.

And if you wish for another still greater proof of his genius and wisdom look at this Catholic Church that he founded, its ranks and constitution, its rites and sacraments.

Now in the third place, far higher than beauty of the body, higher than genius and wisdom the beauty of the mind, comes the beauty of his character, his character as man. For the most part his very enemies, those that do not believe in him, allow that a character so noble was never seen in human mould. Plato the heathen, the greatest of the Greek philosophers, foretold of him: he drew by his wisdom a picture of the just man in his justice crucified and it was fulfilled in Christ. Poor was his station, laborious his life, bitter his ending: through poverty, through labour, through crucifixion his majesty of nature more shines. No heart as his was ever so tender, but tenderness was not all: this heart so tender was as brave, it could be stern. He found the thought of his Passion past bearing, yet he went through with it. He was feared when he chose: he took a whip and single-handed cleared the temple. The thought of his gentleness towards children, towards the afflicted, towards sinners, is often dwelt on; that of his courage less. But for my part I like to feel that I should have feared him. We hear also of his love, as for John and Lazarus; and even love at first sight, as of the young man that had kept all the commandments from his childhood. But he warned or rebuked his best friends when need was, as Peter, Martha, and even his mother. For, as St. John says, he was full both of grace and of truth.

But, brethren, from all that might be said of his character I single out one point and beg you to notice that. He loved to praise, he loved to reward. He knew what was in man, he best knew men's faults and yet he was the warmest in their praise. When he worked a miracle he would grace it with "Thy faith hath saved thee," that it might almost seem the receiver's work, not his. He said of Nathaniel that he was an Israelite without guile; he that searches hearts said this, and yet what praise that was to give! He called the two sons of Zebedee Sons of Thunder, kind and stately and honourable name! We read of nothing thunderlike that they did except, what was sinful, to wish fire down from heaven on some sinners but they deserved the name or he would not have given it, and he has given it them for all time. Of John the Baptist he said that his greater was not born of women. He said to Peter, "Thou art Rock," and rewarded a moment's acknowledgment of him with the lasting headship of his Church. He defended [Mary] Magdalen and took means that the story of her generosity should be told forever. And though he bids *us* say we are unprofitable servants, yet he himself will say to each of us, "Good and faithful servant, well done."

A Short Introduction
to the Poems

The following was published as the preface to Hopkins's posthumously published poems in 1918. It was probably written in the early 1880s and was obviously never polished by the author into a final form. It does, however, provide some insight into the unusual rhythm in his poems.

Excerpts from Hopkins's
Writings about Poetry

The poems in this book are written some in Running Rhythm, the common rhythm in English use, some in Sprung Rhythm, and some in a mixture of the two. And those in the common rhythm are some counterpointed, some not.

Common English rhythm, called Running Rhythm above, is measured by feet of either two or three syllables and (putting aside the imperfect feet at the beginning and end of lines and also some unusual measures in which feet seem to be paired together and double or composite feet to arise) never more or less.

Every foot has one principal stress or accent, and this or the syllable it falls on may be called the Stress of the foot and the other part, the one or two unaccented syllables, the Slack. Feet (and the rhythms made out of them) in which the Stress comes first are called Falling Feet and Falling Rhythms, feet and rhythm in which the Slack comes first are called Rising Feet and Rhythms, and if the Stress is between two Slacks there will be Rocking Feet and Rhythms. These distinctions are real and true to nature; but for purposes of scanning it is a great convenience to follow the example of music and take the stress always first, as the accent or the chief accent always comes first in a musical bar. If this is done there will be in common English verse only two possible feet—the so-called accentual Trochee and Dactyl, and correspondingly only two possible uniform rhythms, the so-called Trochaic and Dactylic. But they may be mixed and then what the Greeks called a Logaoedic Rhythm arises. These are the facts and according to these the scanning of ordinary regularly-written English verse is very simple indeed and to bring in other principles is here unnecessary.

But because verse written strictly in these feet and by these principles will become same and tame the poets have brought in licences and departures from rule to give variety, and especially when the natural rhythm is rising, as in the common ten-syllable or five-foot verse, rhymed or blank. These irregularities are chiefly Reversed Feet and Reversed or Counterpoint Rhythm, which two things are two steps or degrees of licence in the same kind. By a reversed foot I mean the putting the stress where, to judge by the rest of the measure, the slack should be and the slack where the stress, and this is done freely at the beginning of a line and, in the course of a line, after a pause; only scarcely ever in the second foot or place and never in the last, unless when the poet designs some extraordinary effect; for these places are characteristic and sensitive and cannot well be touched. But the reversal of the first foot and of some middle foot after a strong pause is a thing so natural that our poets have generally done it, from Chaucer down, without remark and it commonly passes unnoticed and cannot be said to amount to a formal change of rhythm, but rather is that irregularity which all natural growth and motion shews. If however the reversal is repeated in two feet running, especially so as to include the sensitive second foot, it must be due either to great want of ear or else is a calculated effect, the superinducing or *mounting* of a new rhythm upon the old; and since the new or mounted rhythm is actually heard and at the same time the mind naturally supplies the natural or standard foregoing rhythm, for we do not forget what the rhythm is that by rights we should be hearing, two rhythms are in some manner running at once and we have something answerable to counterpoint in music, which is two or more strains of tune going on together, and this is Counterpoint Rhythm. Of this kind of verse Milton is the great master and the choruses of *Samson Agonistes* are written throughout in it—but with the disadvantage that he does not let the reader clearly know what the ground-rhythm is meant to be and so they have struck most readers as merely irregular. And in fact if you counterpoint throughout, since one only of the counter rhythms is actually heard, the other is really destroyed or cannot come to exist and what is written is one rhythm only and probably Sprung Rhythm, of which I now speak.

Sprung Rhythm, as used in this book, is measured by feet of from one to four syllables, regularly, and for particular effects any number of weak or slack syllables may be used. It has one stress, which falls on the only syllable, if there is only one, or, if there are more, then scanning as above, on the first, and so gives rise to four sorts of feet, a monosyllable and the so-called accentual Trochee, Dactyl, and the First Paeon. And there will be four corresponding natural rhythms; but nominally the feet are mixed and any one may follow any other. And hence Sprung Rhythm differs from Running Rhythm in having or being only one nominal rhythm, a mixed or "logaoedic" one, instead of three, but on the other hand in having twice the flexibility of foot, so that any two stresses may either follow one another running or be divided by one, two, or three slack syllables. But strict Sprung Rhythm cannot be counterpointed. In Sprung Rhythm, as in logaoedic rhythm generally, the feet are assumed to be equally long or strong and their seeming inequality is made up by pause or stressing.

Remark also that it is natural in Sprung Rhythm for the lines to be *rove over,* that is for the scanning of each line immediately to take up that of the one before, so that if the first has one or more syllables at its end the other must have so many the less at its beginning; and in fact the scanning runs on without break from the beginning, say, of a stanza to the end and all the stanza is one long strain, though written in lines asunder.

Two licences are natural to Sprung Rhythm. The one is rests, as in music; but of this an example is scarcely to be found in this book, unless in the *Echos,* second line. The other is *hangers* or *outrides,* that is one, two, or three slack syllables added to a foot and not counting in the nominal scanning. They are so called because they seem to hang below the line or ride forward or backward from it in another dimension than the line itself, according to a principle needless to explain here. These outriding half feet or hangers are marked by a loop underneath them, and plenty of them will be found.

The other marks are easily understood, namely accents, where the reader might be in doubt which syllable should have the stress; slurs, that is loops over syllables, to tie them together into the time of one; little loops at the end of a line to shew that the rhyme goes on to the first letter of the next line; what in music are called pauses ⌒, to shew that the syllable should be dwelt on; and twirls ∿, to mark reversed or counterpointed rhythm.

Note on the nature and history of Sprung Rhythm— Sprung Rhythm is the most natural of things. For (1) it is the rhythm of common speech and of written prose, when rhythm is perceived in them. (2) It is the rhythm of all but the most monotonously regular music, so that in the words of choruses and refrains and in songs written closely to music it arises. (3) It is found in nursery rhymes, weather saws, and so on; because, however these may have been once made in running rhythm, the terminations having dropped off by the change of language, the stresses come together and so the rhythm is sprung. (4) It arises in common verse when reversed or counterpointed, for the same reason.

But nevertheless in spite of all this and though Greek and Latin lyric verse, which is well known, and the old English verse seen in *Pierce Ploughman* are in sprung rhythm, it has in fact ceased to be used since the Elizabethan age, Greene being the last writer who can be said to have recognised it. For perhaps there was not, down to our days, a single, even short, poem in English in which sprung rhythm is employed—not for single effects or in fixed places—but as the governing principle of the scansion. I say this because the contrary has been asserted: if it is otherwise the poem should be cited.

From Robert Bridges's Preface to the 1918 Edition

An editor of posthumous work is bounden to give some account of the authority for his text; and it is the purpose of the following notes to satisfy inquiry concerning matters whereof the present editor has the advantage of first-hand or particular knowledge.

The sources are four, and will be distinguished as A, B, D, and H, as here described. A is my own collection, a MS. book made up of autographs—by which word I denote poems in the author's handwriting—pasted into it as they were received from him, and also of contemporary copies of other poems. These autographs and copies date from '67 to '89, the year of his death. Additions made by copying after that date are not reckoned or used....

B is a MS. book, into which, in '83, I copied from A certain poems of which the author had kept no copy. He was remiss in making fair copies of his work, and his autograph of *The Deutschland* having been (seemingly) lost, I copied that poem and others from A at his request. After that date he entered more poems in this book as he completed them, and he also made both corrections of copy and emendations of the poems which had been copied into it by me. Thus, if a poem occur in both A and B, then B is the later and, except for overlooked errors of copyist, the better authority. The last entry written by G. M. H. into this book is of the date 1887.

D is a collection of the author's letters to Canon Dixon, the only other friend who ever read his poems, with but few exceptions whether of persons or of poems. These letters are in my keeping; they contain autographs of a few poems with late corrections.

H is the bundle of posthumous papers that came into my hands at the author's death. These were at the time examined, sorted, and indexed; and the more important pieces—of which copies were taken—were inserted into a scrap-book. That collection is the source of a series of his most mature sonnets, and of almost all the unfinished poems and fragments. Among these papers were also some early drafts....

The latest autographs and autographic corrections have been preferred. In the very few instances in which this principle was overruled, as in Nos. 1 and 27, the justification will be found in the note to the poem. The finished poems from 1 to 51 are ranged chronologically by the years, but in the section 52–74 a fanciful grouping of the fragments was preferred to the inevitable misrepresentations of conjectural dating. G. M. H. dated his poems from their inception, and however much he revised a poem he would date his recast as his first draft. Thus *Handsome Heart* was written and sent to me in '79; and the recast, which I reject, was not made before '83, while the final corrections may be some years later; and yet his last autograph is dated as the first "Oxford '79."

This edition purports to convey all the author's serious mature poems; and he would probably not have wished any of his earlier poems nor so many of his fragments to have been included. Of the former class three specimens only are admitted—and these, which may be considered of exceptional merit or interest, had already been given to the public—but of the latter almost everything; because these scraps being of mature date, generally contain some special beauty of thought or diction, and are invariably of metrical or rhythmical interest: some of them are in this respect as remarkable as anything in the volume. As for exclusion, no translations of any kind are published here, whether into Greek or Latin from the English—of which there are autographs and copies in A—or the Englishing of Latin hymns—occurring in H—: these last are not in my opinion of special merit; and with them I class a few religious pieces which will be noticed later.

Of the peculiar scheme of prosody invented and developed by the author a full account is out of the question. His own preface together with his description of the metrical scheme of each poem—which is always, wherever it exists, transcribed in the notes—may be a sufficient guide for practical purposes. Moreover, the intention of the rhythm, in places where it might seem doubtful, has been indicated by accents printed over the determining syllables: in the later poems these accents correspond generally with the author's own marks; in the earlier poems they do not, but are trustworthy translations.

It was at one time the author's practice to use a very elaborate system of marks, all indicating the speech-movement: the autograph (in A) of *Harry Ploughman* carries seven different marks, each one defined at the foot. When reading through his letters for the purpose of determining dates, I noted a few sentences on this subject which will justify the method that I have followed in the text. In 1883 he wrote: "You were right to leave out the marks: they were not consistent for one thing, and are always offensive. Still there must be some. Either I must invent a notation applied throughout as in music or else I must only mark where the reader is likely to mistake, and for the present this is what I shall do." And again in '85: "This is my difficulty, what marks to use and when to use them: they are so much needed and yet so objectionable. About punctuation my mind is clear: I can give a rule for everything I write myself, and even for other people, though they might not agree with me perhaps." In this last matter the autographs are rigidly respected, the rare intentional aberration being scrupulously noted. And so I have respected his indentation of the verse; but in the sonnets, while my indentation corresponds, as a rule, with some autograph, I have felt free to consider conveniences, following, however, his growing practice to eschew it altogether.

Apart from questions of taste—and if these poems were to be arraigned for errors of what may he called taste, they might be convicted of occasional affectation in metaphor, as where the hills are "as a stallion stalwart, very-violet-sweet," or of some perversion of human feeling, as, for instance, the "nostrils' relish of incense along the sanctuary side," or "the Holy Ghost with warm breast and with ah! bright wings," these and a few such examples are mostly efforts to force emotion into theological or sectarian channels, as in "the comfortless unconfessed" and the unpoetic line "His mystery must be unstressed stressed," or, again, the exaggerated Marianism of some pieces, or the naked encounter of sensualism and asceticism which hurts the "Golden Echo."

Apart, I say, from such faults of taste, which few as they numerically are yet affect my liking and more repel my sympathy than do all the rude shocks of his purely artistic wantonness—apart from these there are definite faults of style which a reader must have courage to face, and must in some measure condone before he can discover the great beauties. For these blemishes in the poet's style are of such quality and magnitude as to deny him even a hearing from those who love a continuous literary decorum and are grown to be intolerant of its absence. And it is well to be clear that there is no pretence to reverse the condemnation of those faults, for which the poet has duly suffered. The extravagances are and will remain what they were. Nor can credit be gained from pointing them out: yet, to put readers at their ease, I will here define them: they may be called Oddity and Obscurity; and since the first may provoke laughter when a writer is serious (and this poet is always serious), while the latter must prevent him from being understood (and this poet has always something to say), it may be assumed that they were not a part of his intention. Something of what he thought on this subject may be seen in the following extracts from his letters. In Feb.

1879, he wrote: "All therefore that I think of doing is to keep my verses together in one place—at present I have not even correct copies—, that, if anyone should like, they might be published after my death. And that again is unlikely, as well as remote.... No doubt my poetry errs on the side of oddness. I hope in time to have a more balanced and Miltonic style. But as air, melody, is what strikes me most of all in music and design in painting, so design, pattern, or what I am in the habit of calling *inscape* is what I above all aim at in poetry. Now it is the virtue of design, pattern, or inscape to be distinctive and it is the vice of distinctiveness to become queer. This vice I cannot have escaped." And again two months later: "Moreover the oddness may make them repulsive at first and yet Lang might have liked them on a second reading. Indeed when, on somebody returning me the *Eurydice,* I opened and read some lines, as one commonly reads whether prose or verse, with the eyes, so to say, only, it struck me aghast with a kind of raw nakedness and unmitigated violence I was unprepared for: but take breath and read it with the ears, as I always wish to be read, and my verse becomes all right."

As regards Oddity then, it is plain that the poet was himself fully alive to it, but he was not sufficiently aware of his obscurity, and he could not understand why his friends found his sentences so difficult: he would never have believed that, among all the ellipses and liberties of his grammar, the one chief cause is his habitual omission of the relative pronoun; and yet this is so, and the examination of a simple example or two may serve a general purpose.

This grammatical liberty, though it is a common convenience in conversation and has therefore its proper place in good writing, is apt to confuse the parts of speech, and to reduce a normal sequence of words to mere jargon. Writers who carelessly rely on their elliptical speech-forms to govern the elaborate sentences of their literary composition little know what a conscious effort of interpretation they often impose on their readers. But it was not carelessness in Gerard Hopkins: he had full skill and practice and scholarship in conventional forms, and it is easy to see that he banished these purely constructional syllables from his verse because they took up room which he thought he could not afford them: he needed in his scheme all his space for his poetical words, and he wished those to crowd out every merely grammatical colourless or toneless element; and so when he had got into the habit of doing without these relative pronouns—though he must, I suppose, have supplied them in his thought,—he abuses the licence beyond precedent, as when he writes (No. 17) "O Hero savest!" for "O Hero that Savest!"

Another example of this (from the 5th stanza of No. 23) will discover another cause of obscurity; the line "Squander the hell-rook ranks sally to molest him" means "Scatter the ranks that sally to molest him": but since the words *squander* and *sally* occupy similar positions in the two sections of the verse, and are enforced by a similar accentuation, the second verb deprived of its pronoun will follow the first and appear as an imperative; and there is nothing to prevent its being so taken but the contradiction that it makes in the meaning; whereas the grammar should expose and enforce the meaning, not have to be determined by the meaning. Moreover, there is no way of enunciating this line which will avoid the confusion; because if, knowing that *sally* should not have the same intonation as *squander,* the reader mitigates the accent, and in doing so lessens or obliterates the caesural pause which exposes its accent, then *ranks* becomes a genitive and *sally* a substantive.

Here, then, is another source of the poet's obscurity; that in aiming at condensation he neglects the need that there is for care in the placing of words that are grammatically ambiguous. English swarms with words that have one identical form for substantive, adjective, and verb; and such a word should never be so placed as to allow of any doubt as to what part of speech it is used for; because such ambiguity or momentary uncertainty destroys the force of the sentence. Now our author not only neglects this essential propriety but he would seem even to welcome and seek artistic effect in the consequent confusion; and he will sometimes so arrange such words that a reader looking for a verb may find that he has two or three ambiguous monosyllables from which to select, and must be in doubt as to which promises best to give any meaning that he can welcome; and then, after his choice is made, he may be left with some homeless monosyllable still on his hands. Nor is our author apparently sensitive to the irrelevant suggestions that our numerous homophones cause; and he will provoke further ambiguities or obscurities by straining the meaning of these unfortunate words.

Finally, the rhymes where they are peculiar are often repellent, and so far from adding charm to the verse that they appear as obstacles. This must not blind one from recognizing that Gerard Hopkins, where he is simple and straightforward in his rhyme is a master of it—there are many instances—but when he indulges in freaks, his childishness is incredible. His intention in such places is that the verses should be recited running on without pause, and the rhyme occurring in their midst should be like a phonetic accident, merely satisfying the prescribed form. But his phonetic rhymes are often indefensible on his own principle. The rhyme to *communion* in "The Bugler" is hideous, and the suspicion that the poet thought it ingenious is appalling; *eternal,* in "The Eurydice," does not correspond with *burn all,* and in "Felix Randal" *and some* and *handsome* is as truly an eye-rhyme as the *love* and *prove* which he despised and abjured;—and it is more distressing, because the old-fashioned conventional eye-rhymes are accepted as such without speech-adaptation, and to many ears are a pleasant relief from the fixed jingle of the perfect rhyme; whereas his false ear-rhymes ask to have their slight but indispensable differences obliterated in the reading, and thus they expose their defect, which is of a disagreeable and vulgar or even comic quality. He did not escape full criticism and ample ridicule for such things in his lifetime; and in '83 he wrote: "Some of my rhymes I regret, but they are past changing, grubs in amber: there are only a few of these; others are unassailable; some others again there are which malignity may munch at but the Muses love."

Now these are bad faults, and, as I said, a reader, if he is to get any enjoyment from the author's genius, must be somewhat tolerant of them; and they have a real relation to the means whereby the very forcible and original effects of beauty are produced. There is nothing stranger in these poems than the mixture of passages of extreme delicacy and exquisite diction with passages where, in a jungle of rough root-words, emphasis seems to oust euphony; and both these qualities, emphasis and euphony, appear in their extreme forms. It was an idiosyncrasy of this student's mind to push everything to its logical extreme, and take pleasure in a paradoxical result; as may be seen in his prosody where a simple theory seems to be used only as a basis for unexampled liberty. He was flattered when I called him, and saw the humour of it—and one would expect to find in his work the force of emphatic condensation and the magic of melodious expression, both in their extreme forms. Now since those who study style in itself must allow a proper place to the emphatic expression, this experiment, which supplies as novel examples of success as of failure, should be full of interest; and such interest will promote tolerance.

[One] fragment ... is the draft of what appears to be an attempt to explain how an artist has not free-will in his creation. He works out his own nature instinctively as he happens to be made, and is irresponsible for the result. It is lamentable that Gerard Hopkins died when, to judge by his latest work, he was beginning to concentrate the force of all his luxuriant experiments in rhythm and diction, and castigate his art into a more reserved style. Few will read the terrible posthumous sonnets without such high admiration and respect for his poetical power as must lead them to search out the rare masterly beauties that distinguish his work.

The Poems

The Caged Skylark

As a dare-gale skylark scanted in a dull cage
　Man's mounting spirit in his bone-house, mean house,
　　　dwells—
　That bird beyond the remembering his free falls,
This in drudgery, day-labouring-out life's age.

Though aloft on turf or perch or poor low stage,
　Both sing sometimes the sweetest, sweetest spells,
　Yet both droop deadly sómetimes in their cells
Or wring their barriers in bursts of fear or rage.

Not that the sweet-fowl, song-fowl, needs no rest—
Why, hear him, hear him babble and drop down to
　　　his nest,
　But his own nest, wild nest, no prison.

Man's spirit will be flesh-bound when found at best,
But uncumberèd: meadow-down is not distressed
　For a rainbow footing it nor he for his bónes rísen.

Before reading the final three lines of this poem, John Pick reflects,
"Such lines would seem to consider the flesh as a cage, a prison for
the soul, the spirit anxious to find freedom from its bondage. But
the final lines make clear that this is true only until the ideal rela-
tionship (when the cage is no cage, the prison no prison) is attained.
And the dogmas of the Incarnation, the Resurrection, as well as the
whole liturgical worship of the Church, have constantly reasserted
the sanctity of the body, the holiness of the senses."[5]

Duns Scotus's Oxford

Towery city and branchy between towers;
Cuckoo-echoing, bell-swarmèd, lark-charmèd, rook-
      racked, river-rounded;
The dapple-eared lily below thee; that country and
      town did
Once encounter in, here coped and poisèd powers;

Thou hast a base and brickish skirt there, sours
That neighbour-nature thy grey beauty is grounded
Best in; graceless growth, thou hast confounded
Rural rural keeping—folk, flocks, and flowers.

Yet ah! this air I gather and I release
He lived on; these weeds and waters, these walls are what
He haunted who of all men most sways my spirits to
      peace;

Of realty the rarest-veinèd unraveller; a not
Rivalled insight, be rival Italy or Greece;
Who fired France for Mary without spot.

Johannes Duns Scotus (1266–1308) was an Oxford philosopher
whose teaching was so astute and sublime that he gained the name
"the Subtle Doctor." As a student at Oxford centuries later,
Hopkins first read Scotus's writings and became, he wrote, "flush
with a new stroke of enthusiasm. It may come to nothing or it may
be a mercy from God. But just then when I took in any inscape of
the sky or sea I thought of Scotus."[6]

At the Wedding March

God with honour hang your head,
Groom, and grace you, bride, your bed
With lissome scions, sweet scions,
Out of hallowed bodies bred.

Each be other's comfort kind:
Déep, déeper than divined,
Divine charity, dear charity,
Fast you ever, fast bind.

Then let the March tread our ears:
I to him turn with tears
Who to wedlock, his wonder wedlock,
Déals tríumph and immortal years.

The Blessed Virgin compared to the Air we Breathe

Wild air, world-mothering air,
Nestling me everywhere,
That each eyelash or hair
Girdles; goes home betwixt
The fleeciest, frailest-flixed
Snowflake; that's fairly mixed
With, riddles, and is rife
In every least thing's life;
This needful, never spent,
And nursing element;
My more than meat and drink,
My meal at every wink;
This air, which, by life's law,
My lung must draw and draw
Now but to breathe its praise,
Minds me in many ways
Of her who not only
Gave God's infinity
Dwindled to infancy
Welcome in womb and breast,
Birth, milk, and all the rest
But mothers each new grace
That does now reach our race—
Mary Immaculate,
Merely a woman, yet
Whose presence, power is
Great as no goddess's

Was deemèd, dreamèd; who
This one work has to do—
Let all God's glory through,
God's glory which would go
Through her and from her flow
Off, and no way but so.
　　I say that we are wound
With mercy round and round
As if with air: the same
Is Mary, more by name.
She, wild web, wondrous robe,
Mantles the guilty globe,
Since God has let dispense
Her prayers his providence:
Nay, more than almoner,
The sweet alms' self is her
And men are meant to share
Her life as life does air.
　　If I have understood,
She holds high motherhood
Towards all our ghostly good
And plays in grace her part
About man's beating heart,
Laying, like air's fine flood,
The deathdance in his blood;
Yet no part but what will
Be Christ our Saviour still.
Of her flesh he took flesh:

He does take fresh and fresh,
Though much the mystery how,
Not flesh but spirit now
And makes, O marvellous!
New Nazareths in us,
Where she shall yet conceive
Him, morning, noon, and eve;
New Bethlems, and he born
There, evening, noon, and morn—
Bethlem or Nazareth,
Men here may draw like breath
More Christ and baffle death;
Who, born so, comes to be
New self and nobler me
In each one and each one
More makes, when all is done,
Both God's and Mary's Son.
    Again, look overhead
How air is azuрèd;
O how! Nay do but stand
Where you can lift your hand
Skywards: rich, rich it laps
Round the four fingergaps.
Yet such a sapphire-shot,
Charged, steepèd sky will not
Stain light. Yea, mark you this:
It does no prejudice.

The glass-blue days are those
When every colour glows,
Each shape and shadow shows.
Blue be it: this blue heaven
The seven or seven times seven
Hued sunbeam will transmit
Perfect, not alter it.
Or if there does some soft,
On things aloof, aloft,
Bloom breathe, that one breath more
Earth is the fairer for.
Whereas did air not make
This bath of blue and slake
His fire, the sun would shake,
A blear and blinding ball
With blackness bound, and all
The thick stars round him roll
Flashing like flecks of coal,
Quartz-fret, or sparks of salt,
In grimy vasty vault.
  So God was god of old:
A mother came to mould
Those limbs like ours which are
What must make our daystar
Much dearer to mankind;
Whose glory bare would blind
Or less would win man's mind.

Through her we may see him
Made sweeter, not made dim,
And her hand leaves his light
Sifted to suit our sight.

Be thou then, O thou dear
Mother, my atmosphere;
My happier world, wherein
To wend and meet no sin;
Above me, round me lie
Fronting my froward eye
With sweet and scarless sky;
Stir in my ears, speak there
Of God's love, O live air,
Of patience, penance, prayer:
Worldmothering air, air wild,
Wound with thee, in thee isled,
Fold home, fast fold thy child.

As Kingfishers Catch Fire

As kingfishers catch fire, dragonflies draw flame;
  As tumbled over rim in roundy wells
  Stones ring; like each tucked string tells, each hung
      bell's
Bow swung finds tongue to fling out broad its name;
Each mortal thing does one thing and the same:
  Deals out that being indoors each one dwells;
  Selves—goes itself; *myself* it speaks and spells,
Crying *What I do is me: for that I came.*

Í say more: the just man justices;
  Keeps gráce: thát keeps all his goings graces;
Acts in God's eye what in God's eye he is—
  Chríst. For Christ plays in ten thousand places,
Lovely in limbs, and lovely in eyes not his
  To the Father through the features of men's faces.

Binsey Poplars

felled 1879

My aspens dear, whose airy cages quelled,
Quelled or quenched in leaves the leaping sun,
All felled, felled, are all felled;
    Of a fresh and following folded rank
        Not spared, not one
        That dandled a sandalled
        Shadow that swam or sank
On meadow and river and wind-wandering
    weed-winding bank.

O if we but knew what we do
        When we delve or hew—
    Hack and rack the growing green!
      Since country is so tender
    To touch, her being só slender,
    That, like this sleek and seeing ball
    But a prick will make no eye at all,
    Where we, even where we mean
        To mend her we end her,
      When we hew or delve:
After-comers cannot guess the beauty been.
    Ten or twelve, only ten or twelve
      Strokes of havoc únselve
      The sweet especial scene,
     Rural scene, a rural scene,
     Sweet especial rural scene.

God's Grandeur

The world is charged with the grandeur of God.
  It will flame out, like shining from shook foil;
  It gathers to a greatness, like the ooze of oil
Crushed. Why do men then now not reck his rod?
Generations have trod, have trod, have trod;
  And all is seared with trade; bleared, smeared with
      toil;
  And wears man's smudge and shares man's smell:
      the soil
Is bare now, nor can foot feel, being shod.

And, for all this, nature is never spent;
  There lives the dearest freshness deep down things;
And though the last lights off the black West went
  Oh, morning, at the brown brink eastward,
      springs—
Because the Holy Ghost over the bent
  World broods with warm breast and with ah! bright
      wings.

Hopkins wrote, in his own commentary for this poem: "God is so
deeply present to everything that it would be impossible for him
but for his infinity not to be identified with them or, from the other
side, impossible but for his infinity so to be present to them. This is
oddly expressed, I see; I mean—a being so intimately present as
God is to other things would be identified with them were it not for
God's infinity or were it not for God's infinity he could not be so
intimately present to things."[7]

I Wake and Feel the Fell of Dark

I wake and feel the fell of dark, not day.
What hours, O what black hoürs we have spent
This night! what sights you, heart, saw; ways you
       went!
And more must, in yet longer light's delay.

With witness I speak this. But where I say
Hours I mean years, mean life. And my lament
Is cries countless, cries like dead letters sent
To dearest him that lives alas! away.

I am gall, I am heartburn. God's most deep decree
Bitter would have me taste: my taste was me;
Bones built in me, flesh filled, blood brimmed the
       curse.

Selfyeast of spirit a dull dough sours. I see
The lost are like this, and their scourge to be
As I am mine, their sweating selves; but worse.

Pied Beauty

Glory be to God for dappled things—
   For skies of couple-colour as a brinded cow;
     For rose-moles all in stipple upon trout that swim;
Fresh-firecoal chestnut-falls; finches' wings;
   Landscape plotted and pieced—fold, fallow, and
      plough;
     And áll trádes, their gear and tackle and trim.

All things counter, original, spare, strange;
   Whatever is fickle, freckled (who knows how?)
     With swift, slow; sweet, sour; adazzle, dim;
He fathers-forth whose beauty is past change:
                  Praise him.

The Starlight Night

Look at the stars! look, look up at the skies!
  O look at all the fire-folk sitting in the air!
  The bright boroughs, the circle-citadels there!
Down in dim woods the diamond delves! the elves'-
      eyes!
The grey lawns cold where gold, where quickgold
      lies!
  Wind-beat whitebeam! airy abeles set on a flare!
  Flake-doves sent floating forth at a farmyard scare!—
Ah well! it is all a purchase, all is a prize.
Buy then! bid then!—What?—Prayer, patience,
      alms, vows.
Look, look: a May-mess, like on orchard boughs!
  Look! March-bloom, like on mealed-with-yellow
      sallows!
These are indeed the barn; withindoors house
The shocks. This piece-bright paling shuts the spouse
  Christ home, Christ and his mother and all his
      hallows.

In the Valley of the Elwy

I remember a house where all were good
  To me, God knows, deserving no such thing:
  Comforting smell breathed at very entering,
Fetched fresh, as I suppose, off some sweet wood.

That cordial air made those kind people a hood
  All over, as a bevy of eggs the mothering wing
  Will, or mild nights the new morsels of Spring:
Why, it seemed of course; seemed of right it should.

Lovely the woods, waters, meadows, combes, vales,
All the air things wear that build this world of Wales;
  Only the inmate does not correspond:

God, lover of souls, swaying considerate scales,
Complete thy creature dear O where it fails,
  Being mighty a master, being a father and fond.

The Windhover:

To Christ our Lord

I caught this morning morning's minion, king-
  dom of daylight's dauphin, dapple-dawn-drawn Falcon,
      in his riding
  Of the rolling level underneath him steady air, and
      striding
High there, how he rung upon the rein of a wimpling
      wing
In his ecstasy! then off, off forth on swing,
  As a skate's heel sweeps smooth on a bow-bend: the hurl
      and gliding
  Rebuffed the big wind. My heart in hiding
Stirred for a bird,—the achieve of, the mastery of the
      thing!

Brute beauty and valour and act, oh, air, pride, plume, here
  Buckle! AND the fire that breaks from thee then, a billion
Times told lovelier, more dangerous, O my chevalier!

  No wonder of it: shéer plód makes plough down sillion
Shine, and blue-bleak embers, ah my dear,
  Fall, gall themselves, and gash gold-vermillion.

"The Windhover" was said to be Hopkins's favorite of his own poems.

Ribblesdale

Earth, sweet Earth, sweet landscape, with leavès
     throng
And louchèd low grass, heaven that dost appeal
To, with no tongue to plead, no heart to feel;
That canst but only be, but dost that long—

Thou canst but be, but that thou well dost; strong
Thy plea with him who dealt, nay does now deal,
Thy lovely dale down thus and thus bids reel
Thy river, and o'er gives all to rack or wrong.

And what is Earth's eye, tongue, or heart else, where
Else, but in dear and dogged man?—Ah, the heir
To his own selfbent so bound, so tied to his turn,

To thriftless reave both our rich round world bare
And none reck of world after, this bids wear
Earth brows of such care, care and dear concern.

Spring

Nothing is so beautiful as Spring—
   When weeds, in wheels, shoot long and lovely and
      lush;
   Thrush's eggs look little low heavens, and thrush
Through the echoing timber does so rinse and wring
The ear, it strikes like lightnings to hear him sing;
   The glassy peartree leaves and blooms, they brush
   The descending blue; that blue is all in a rush
With richness; the racing lambs too have fair their
      fling.

What is all this juice and all this joy?
   A strain of the earth's sweet being in the beginning
In Eden garden.—Have, get, before it cloy,

   Before it cloud, Christ, lord, and sour with sinning,
Innocent mind and Mayday in girl and boy,
   Most, O maid's child, thy choice and worthy the
      winning.

The May Magnificat

May is Mary's month, and I
Muse at that and wonder why:
    Her feasts follow reason,
    Dated due to season—

Candlemas, Lady Day;
But the Lady Month, May,
    Why fasten that upon her,
    With a feasting in her honour?

Is it only its being brighter
Than the most are must delight her?
    Is it opportunest
    And flowers finds soonest?

Ask of her, the mighty mother:
Her reply puts this other
    Question: What is Spring?—
    Growth in every thing—

Flesh and fleece, fur and feather,
Grass and greenworld all together;
    Star-eyed strawberry-breasted
    Throstle above her nested

Cluster of bugle blue eggs thin
Forms and warms the life within;
    And bird and blossom swell
    In sod or sheath or shell.

All things rising, all things sizing
Mary sees, sympathising
    With that world of good,
Nature's motherhood.

Their magnifying of each its kind
With delight calls to mind
    How she did in her stored
    Magnify the Lord.

Well but there was more than this:
Spring's universal bliss
    Much, had much to say
    To offering Mary May.

When drop-of-blood-and-foam-dapple
Bloom lights the orchard-apple
    And thicket and thorp are merry
    With silver-surfèd cherry

And azuring-over greybell makes
Wood banks and brakes wash wet like lakes
 And magic cuckoocall
 Caps, clears, and clinches all—

This ecstasy all through mothering earth
Tells Mary her mirth till Christ's birth
 To remember and exultation
 In God who was her salvation.

Hurrahing in Harvest

Summer ends now; now, barbarous in beauty, the
      stooks rise
Around; up above, what wind-walks! what lovely
      behaviour
Of silk-sack clouds! has wilder, wilful-wavier
Meal-drift moulded ever and melted across skies?

I walk, I lift up, I lift up heart, eyes,
Down all that glory in the heavens to glean our
      Saviour;
And, éyes, heárt, what looks, what lips yet gave you a
Rapturous love's greeting of realer, of rounder
      replies?

And the azurous hung hills are his world-wielding
      shoulder
Majestic—as a stallion stalwart, very-violet-sweet!—
These things, these things were here and but the
      beholder
Wanting; which two when they once meet,
The heart rears wings bold and bolder
And hurls for him, O half hurls earth for him off
      under his feet.

That Nature Is a Heraclitean Fire and of the Comfort of the Resurrection

Cloud-puffball, torn tufts, tossed pillows ǀ flaunt
    forth, then chevy on an air-
built thoroughfare: heaven-roysterers, in gay-gangs ǀ
    they throng; they glitter in marches.
Down roughcast, down dazzling whitewash, ǀ
    wherever an elm arches,
Shivelights and shadowtackle in long ǀ lashes lace,
    lance, and pair.
Delightfully the bright wind boisterous ǀ ropes,
    wrestles, beats earth bare
Of yestertempest's creases; ǀ in pool and rutpeel
    parches
Squandering ooze to squeezed ǀ dough, crust, dust;
    stanches, starches
Squadroned masks and manmarks ǀ treadmire toil
    there
Footfretted in it. Million-fuelèd, ǀ nature's bonfire
    burns on.
But quench her bonniest, dearest ǀ to her, her clearest-
    selvèd spark
Man, how fast his firedint, ǀ his mark on mind, is
    gone!
Both are in an unfathomable, all is in an enormous
    dark
Drowned. O pity and indig ǀ nation! Manshape, that
    shone

Sheer off, disseveral, a star, | death blots black out;
      nor mark
                  Is any of him at all so stark
But vastness blurs and time | beats level. Enough! the
      Resurrection,
A heart's-clarion! Away grief's gasping, | joyless days,
      dejection.
                  Across my foundering deck shone
A beacon, an eternal beam. | Flesh fade, and mortal
      trash
Fall to the residuary worm; | world's wildfire, leave
      but ash:
                  In a flash, at a trumpet crash,
I am all at once what Christ is, | since he was what I
      am, and
This Jack, joke, poor potsherd, | patch, matchwood,
      immortal diamond,
                  Is immortal diamond.

The Wreck of the Deutschland

*To the
happy memory of five Francisan nuns
exiles by the Falck Laws
drowned between midnight and morning of
Dec. 7th, 1875*

PART THE FIRST

1

Thou mastering me
God! giver of breath and bread;
World's strand, sway of the sea;
Lord of living and dead;
Thou hast bound bones and veins in me, fastened
me flesh,
And after it almost unmade, what with dread,
Thy doing: and dost thou touch me afresh?
Over again I feel thy finger and find thee.

2

I did say yes
O at lightning and lashed rod;
Thou heardst me truer than tongue confess
Thy terror, O Christ, O God;
Thou knowest the walls, altar and hour and night:
The swoon of a heart that the sweep and the hurl
of thee trod

Hard down with a horror of height:
And the midriff astrain with leaning of, laced with
      fire of stress.

3

    The frown of his face
    Before me, the hurtle of hell
  Behind, where, where was a, where was a place?
    I whirled out wings that spell
And fled with a fling of the heart to the heart of the
    Host.
My heart, but you were dovewinged, I can tell,
    Carrier-witted, I am bold to boast,
To flash from the flame to the flame then, tower from
    the grace to the grace.

4

    I am soft sift
    In an hourglass—at the wall
  Fast, but mined with a motion, a drift,
    And it crowds and it combs to the fall;
I steady as a water in a well, to a poise, to a pane,
  But roped with, always, all the way down from the
    tall
    Fells or flanks of the voel, a vein
Of the gospel proffer, a pressure, a principle, Christ's

gift.

5

   I kiss my hand
   To the stars, lovely-asunder
  Starlight, wafting him out of it; and
   Glow, glory in thunder;
 Kiss my hand to the dappled-with-damson west:
 Since, tho' he is under the world's splendour and
   wonder,
  His mystery must be instressed, stressed;
For I greet him the days I meet him, and bless when I
  understand.

6

   Not out of his bliss
   Springs the stress felt
  Nor first from heaven (and few know this)
   Swings the stroke dealt—
 Stroke and a stress that stars and storms deliver,
 That guilt is hushed by, hearts are flushed by and
   melt—
  But it rides time like riding a river
(And here the faithful waver, the faithless fable and
  miss).

7

It dates from day
   Of his going in Galilee;
Warm-laid grave of a womb-life grey;
   Manger, maiden's knee;
The dense and the driven Passion, and frightful
      sweat:
Thence the discharge of it, there its swelling to be,
   Though felt before, though in high flood yet—
What none would have known of it, only the heart,
      being hard at bay,

8

Is out with it! Oh,
   We lash with the best or worst
Word last! How a lush-kept plush-capped sloe
   Will, mouthed to flesh-burst,
Gush!—flush the man, the being with it, sour or
      sweet,

Hopkins explains stanza seven: "Though the lightning-stress of
mystical revelation has been felt in all ages, its main discharge into
the world was from the dark cloud of Christ's Passion. It is the
heart in extremity which best understands and proclaims the beauty
and terror of that Sacrifice. Some are forced to cry *How bitter!*
Others taste only the sweetness. But, sour or sweet, the result is

overwhelming conviction."[8]

Brim, in a flash, full!—Hither then, last or first,
    To hero of Calvary, Christ's feet—
Never ask if meaning it, wanting it, warned of it—
    men go.

9

    Be adored among men,
      God, three-numberèd form;
Wring thy rebel, dogged in den,
      Man's malice, with wrecking and storm.
Beyond saying sweet, past telling of tongue,
    Thou art lightning and love, I found it, a winter
      and warm;
    Father and fondler of heart thou hast wrung:
Hast thy dark descending and most art merciful then.

10

    With an anvil-ding
    And with fire in him forge thy will
Or rather, rather then, stealing as Spring
    Through him, melt him but master him still:
Whether at once, as once at a crash Paul,
Or as Austin, a lingering-out swéet skíll,
    Make mercy in all of us, out of us all

Mastery, but be adored, but be adored King.

11

'Some find me a sword; some
The flange and the rail; flame,
Fang, or flood' goes Death on drum,
And storms bugle his fame.
But wé dream we are rooted in earth—Dust!
Flesh falls within sight of us, we, though our flower
the same,
Wave with the meadow, forget that there must
The sour scythe cringe, and the blear share come.

12

On Saturday sailed from Bremen,
American-outward-bound,
Take settler and seamen, tell men with women,
Two hundred souls in the round—
O Father, not under thy feathers nor ever as guessing
The goal was a shoal, of a fourth the doom to be
drowned;
Yet did the dark side of the bay of thy blessing
Not vault them, the million of rounds of thy mercy

not reeve even them in?

13

Into the snows she sweeps,
　　Hurling the haven behind,
　The Deutschland, on Sunday; and so the sky
　　keeps,
　　　For the infinite air is unkind,
And the sea flint-flake, black-backed in the regular
　　blow,
Sitting Eastnortheast, in cursed quarter, the wind;
　Wiry and white-fiery and whírlwind-swivellèd
　　snow
Spins to the widow-making unchilding unfathering
　　deeps.

14

She drove in the dark to leeward,
　　She struck—not a reef or a rock
　But the combs of a smother of sand: night
　　drew her
　　　Dead to the Kentish Knock;
And she beat the bank down with her bows and
　　the ride of her keel:
The breakers rolled on her beam with ruinous shock;
　And canvass and compass, the whorl and the
　　wheel

Idle for ever to waft her or wind her with, these she
    endured.

15

      Hope had grown grey hairs,
      Hope had mourning on,
   Trenched with tears, carved with cares,
      Hope was twelve hours gone;
  And frightful a nightfall folded rueful a day
  Nor rescue, only rocket and light ship, shone,
    And lives at last were washing away:
To the shrouds they took,—they shook in the hurling
    and horrible airs.

16

      One stirred from the rigging to save
      The wild woman-kind below,
   With a rope's end round the man, handy and
    brave—
      He was pitched to his death at a blow,
  For all his dreadnought breast and braids of thew:
  They could tell him for hours, dandled the to and fro
    Through the cobbled foam-fleece. What could
    he do

With the burl of the fountains of air, buck and the
    flood of the wave?

17

    They fought with God's cold—
    And they could not and fell to the deck
  (Crushed them) or water (and drowned them) or
    rolled
    With the sea-romp over the wreck.
Night roared, with the heart-break hearing a heart-
    broke rabble,
The woman's wailing, the crying of child without
    check—
    Till a lioness arose breasting the babble,
A prophetess towered in the tumult, a virginal tongue
    told.

18

    Ah, touched in your bower of bone,
    Are you! turned for an exquisite smart,
  Have you! make words break from me here all
    alone,
    Do you!—mother of being in me, heart.
O unteachably after evil, but uttering truth,
Why, tears! is it? tears; such a melting, a madrigal
    start!

Never-eldering revel and river of youth,
What can it be, this glee? the good you have there of
    your own?

19

    Sister, a sister calling
      A master, her master and mine!—
   And the inboard seas run swirling and hawling;
     The rash smart sloggering brine
  Blinds her; but she that weather sees one thing, one;
  Has one fetch in her: she rears herself to divine
    Ears, and the call of the tall nun
To the men in the tops and the tackle rode over the
    storm's brawling.

20

    She was first of a five and came
      Of a coifèd sisterhood.
  (O Deutschland, double a desperate name!
     O world wide of its good!
 But Gertrude, lily, and Luther, are two of a town,
Christ's lily and beast of the waste wood:

From life's dawn it is drawn down,
Abel is Cain's brother and breasts they have sucked
   the same.)

21

Loathed for a love men knew in them,
   Banned by the land of their birth,
Rhine refused them, Thames would ruin them;
   Surf, snow, river and earth
Gnashed: but thou art above, thou Orion of light;
Thy unchancelling poising palms were weighing
   the worth,
   Thou martyr-master: in thy sight
Storm flakes were scroll-leaved flowers, lily
   showers—sweet heaven was astrew in them.

22

Five! the finding and sake
   And cipher of suffering Christ.
Mark, the mark is of man's make
   And the word of it Sacrificed.
But he scores it in scarlet himself on his own bespoken,
Before-time-taken, dearest prizèd and priced—

Stigma, signal, cinquefoil token
For lettering of the lamb's fleece, ruddying of the
    rose-flake.

23

    Joy fall to thee, father Francis,
    Drawn to the Life that died;
With the gnarls of the nails in thee, niche of the
    lance, his
    Lovescape crucified
And seal of his seraph-arrival! and these thy
    daughters
And five-livèd and leavèd favour and pride,
    Are sisterly sealed in wild waters,
To bathe in his fall-gold mercies, to breathe in his all-
    fire glances.

24

    Away in the loveable west,
    On a pastoral forehead of Wales,
I was under a roof here, I was at rest,
    And they the prey of the gales;
She to the black-about air, to the breaker, the thickly

Falling flakes, to the throng that catches and quails
    Was calling 'O Christ, Christ, come quickly':
The cross to her she calls Christ to her, christens her
    wild-worst Best.

25

    The majesty! what did she mean?
    Breathe, arch and original Breath.
Is it love in her of the being as her lover had
    been?
    Breathe, body of lovely Death.
They were else-minded then, altogether, the men
Woke thee with a *We are perishing* in the weather of
    Gennesareth.
    Or is it that she cried for the crown then,
The keener to come at the comfort for feeling the
    combating keen?

26

    For how to the heart's cheering
    The down-dugged ground-hugged grey
Hovers off, the jay-blue heavens appearing
    Of pied and peeled May!
Blue-beating and hoary-glow height; or night, still
    higher,

With belled fire and the moth-soft Milky Way,
    What by your measure is the heaven of desire,
The treasure never eyesight got, nor was ever guessed
    what for the hearing?

27

    No, but it was not these.
    The jading and jar of the cart,
  Time's tasking, it is fathers that asking for ease
    Of the sodden-with-its-sorrowing heart,
Not danger, electrical horror; then further it finds
The appealing of the Passion is tenderer in prayer
    apart:
    Other, I gather, in measure her mind's
Burden, in wind's burly and beat of endragonèd seas.

28

    But how shall I … make me room there:
    Reach me a … Fancy, come faster—
  Strike you the sight of it? look at it loom there,
    Thing that she … There then! the Master,

Ipse, the only one, Christ, King, Head:
He was to cure the extremity where he had cast her;
Do, deal, lord it with living and dead;
Let him ride, her pride, in his triumph, despatch and
have done with his doom there.

29

Ah! there was a heart right!
There was single eye!
Read the unshapeable shock night
And knew the who and the why;
Wording it how but by him that present and past,
Heaven and earth are word of, worded by?—
The Simon Peter of a soul! to the blast
Tarpeïan-fast, but a blown beacon of light.

30

Jesu, heart's light,
Jesu, maid's son,
What was the feast followed the night

Thou hadst glory of this nun?—
Feast of the one woman without stain.
For so conceivèd, so to conceive thee is done;
 But here was heart-throe, birth of a brain,
Word, that heard and kept thee and uttered thee
  outright.

31

Well, she has thee for the pain, for the
 Patience: but pity of the rest of them!
Heart, go and bleed at a bitterer vein for the
 Comfortless unconfessed of them—
No not uncomforted: lovely-felicitous Providence
Finger of a tender of, O of a feathery delicacy, the
  breast of the
Maiden could obey so, be a bell to, ring of it, and
Startle the poor sheep back! is the shipwrack then a
  harvest, does tempest carry the grain for thee?

32

I admire thee, master of the tides,
 Of the Yore-flood, of the year's fall;
The recurb and the recovery of the gulf's sides,

The girth of it and the wharf of it and the wall;
Staunching, quenching ocean of a motionable mind;
Ground of being, and granite of it: past all
    Grasp God, throned behind
Death with a sovereignty that heeds but hides, bodes
    but abides;

33

With a mercy that outrides
    The all of water, an ark
For the listener; for the lingerer with a love
    glides
    Lower than death and the dark;
A vein for the visiting of the past-prayer, pent in
    prison,
The-last-breath penitent spirits—the uttermost
    mark
    Our passion-plungèd giant risen,
The Christ of the Father compassionate, fetched in
    the storm of his strides.

34

Now burn, new born to the world,
    Doubled-naturèd name,
The heaven-flung, heart-fleshed, maiden-furled
    Miracle-in-Mary-of-flame,

Mid-numberèd he in three of the thunder-throne!
Not a dooms-day dazzle in his coming nor dark as
    he came;
    Kind, but royally reclaiming his own;
A released shower, let flash to the shire, not a
    lightning of fire hard-hurled.

35

    Dame, at our door
    Drowned, and among our shoals,
   Remember us in the roads, the heaven-haven of
    the reward:
    Our King back, Oh, upon English souls!
Let him easter in us, be a dayspring to the dimness
    of us, be a crimson-cresseted east,
More brightening her, rare-dear Britain, as his
    reign rolls,
    Pride, rose, prince, hero of us, high-priest,
Our hearts' charity's hearth's fire, our thoughts'
    chivalry's throng's Lord.

Summa

The best ideal is the true
    And other truth is none,
    All glory be ascribèd to
The holy Three in One.[9]

To what serves Mortal Beauty?

To what serves mortal beauty ˈ —dangerous; does set danc-
ing blood—the O-seal-that-so ˈ feature, flung prouder
form
Than Purcell tune lets tread to? ˈ See: it does this: keeps
warm
Men's wits to the things that are; ˈ what good means—
where a glance
Master more may than gaze, ˈ gaze out of countenance.
Those lovely lads once, wet-fresh ˈ windfalls of war's
storm,
How then should Gregory, a father, ˈ have gleanèd else
from swarm-
èd Rome? But God to a nation ˈ dealt that day's dear
chance.
To man, that needs would worship ˈ block or barren
stone,
Our law says: Love what are ˈ love's worthiest, were all
known;
World's loveliest—men's selves. Self ˈ flashes off frame
and face.
What do then? how meet beauty? ˈ Merely meet it; own,
Home at heart, heaven's sweet gift; ˈ then leave, let that
alone.
Yea, wish that though, wish all, ˈ God's better beauty,
grace.

Notes

1. E. Brett Young, "The Poetry of Gerard Manley Hopkins," *Today* magazine, January 1918.
2. Unsigned review, *Times Literary Supplement* (London), January 9, 1919, 19.
3. Ibid.
4. Unsigned review, *Saturday Westminster Gazette* (London), March 8, 1919, 13.
5. John Pick, *Gerard Manley Hopkins: Priest and Poet* (New York: Oxford University Press, 1942), 70.
6. *Journals and Papers of Gerard Manley Hopkins,* ed. Humphry House and Graham Storey (New York: Oxford University Press, 1959), 221.
7. *Note-books and Papers of Gerard Manley Hopkins,* ed. Humphry House (New York: Oxford University Press, 1937), 316.
8. *Journals and Papers of Gerard Manley Hopkins,* 195.
9. Given here are the first four lines of a sixteen-line poem (publisher's note).

Index of Poems *(by title)*

Index of First Lines

Other Books in
The Mystic Poets Series

HAFIZ

Preface by
Ibrahim Gamard,
member of the Sufi Mevlevi
Order; annotator/translator
of *Rumi and Islam: Selections
from His Stories, Poems, and
Discourses—Annotated &
Explained*

TAGORE

Preface by
Swami Adiswarananda,
Minister and Spiritual
Leader of the
Ramakrishna–
Vivekananda Center of
New York; author of
Meditation & Its Practices

Forthcoming in the Series

HILDEGARD